KINDERKRANKENHAUS

JESI
BENDER

Sagging
Meniscus

The chorus quotes from Ned Lukacher's translation of Jacques Derrida's *Cinders* (University of Nebraska Press, 1991).

© 2021 by Jesi Bender

All Rights Reserved.

Set in Baskerville with LaTeX.

ISBN: 978-1-952386-19-0 (paperback)
Library of Congress Control Number: 2021944397

Sagging Meniscus Press
Montclair, New Jersey
saggingmeniscus.com

For Karlee—Infinite Oracle

"Only in chaos are we conceivable."

—Roberto Bolaño, *2666*

"Each word becomes burdened by an infinite regress of meanings. The word becomes text-manifold, diffuse, scattered over history. And history becomes the horizon of a range of possible contexts."

—Susan Stewart, *Nonsense*

"Let's just say that mankind suffers its language."

—Charles Bernstein, *Girly Man*

"What puts itself in play in this holocaust of play itself?"

—Jacques Derrida, *Cinders*

contents

Kinderkrankenhaus

Dramatis Personae

Dr. Dorothy Schmetterling—Head of KINDERKRANKENHAUS

Mr. & Mrs. Liebschutz—Gnome's parents

Gnome Liebschutz—child patient

the Shadow—child patient

Nix—child patient

Eros—child patient

Cinders—oldest child patient

Python—youngest child patient with white-blond hair

Cinders inside the cave—an adult dressed as child patient Cinders

Gnome Liebschutz inside the cave—an adult dressed as child patient Gnome Liebschutz

Nurse—Assistant to Dr. Schmetterling

Chorus—a group of children, some with the same pageboy haircut, some bald-headed, different races, at least half should have distinctive physical attributes like dwarfism, amelia or meromelia, dyskinesias, etc.

All those playing children are between the ages of 5 and 12.

Setting

Das Kinderkrankenhaus—Hospital in an unknown time and unknown geography, though the audience can hear/smell that it's not far from the sea

1

ACT I · scene 1

{closed curtain}

Stage is edged in sparks.

Chorus, unseen: "*Pure is the word. It calls for fire. Cinders there are, this is what takes place in letting a place occur, so that it will be understood: Nothing will have taken place but the place. Cinders there are: Place there is.*"

{curtain rises}

Interior hallway, das Kinderkrankenhaus.

Mr. & Mrs. Liebschutz exit a large door. Dark set except for lights on characters.

Mr. Liebschutz: "They said you do not need to be concerned. They said everything here is handled with the utmost care."

Mrs. Liebschutz hestitates.

Mr. Liebschutz: "Oh, dear. Please don't get upset."

Mrs. Liebschutz: "It's just—there's something about this whole thing that feels so . . . shameful. Like it's a big secret now."

Mr. Liebschutz: "Secrets aren't shameful, love. Everyone has secrets."

Mrs. Liebschutz turns towards her husband with furrowed brow. He is unnoticing.

Mr. Liebschutz: "It's no one's business."

Mrs.Liebschutz softens, fumbles for words.

Mr. Liebschutz "I know you may have some reservations—but I'm not concerned. We've been over this. I am confident with this decision, leaving it in the skilled hands of Doctor Schmetterling. (Grabbing his wife's wrist) We know this is the right thing to do."

Mrs. Liebschutz: "No, you're right. I know you're right. I guess I just feel like I should feel worse than I do. Leaving a child here all alone."

Mr. Liebschutz: "Alone? No, not alone—there are so many other children in there! Maybe they'll all become friends. Together, they can heal. The doctor says this treatment is the only way to work towards fighting this disease."

Mrs. Liebschutz: "There's no fighting it. It just is."

Mr. Liebschutz pauses. "I said, there's no fighting it; it's done . . . Doctor Schmetterling said they could send us updates if you'd like."

Mrs. Liebschutz, abruptly: "No! No—I want to pretend like this never even happened. A letter would make it too . . ."

Mr. Liebschutz cuts her off: "Okay, well, good. This is for the best."

Mrs. Leibschutz, tears in her eyes: "Yes. It's for the best."

Mr. Liebschutz: "Yes."

They look at each for a moment.

Mr. Liebschutz: "Okay, say goodbye."

He waves at the door.

Mrs. Liebschutz: "Goodbye."

{lights die}

{the beginnings of a fire line the front of the stage like a howl from the horizon}

ACT I · scene 2

{lights rise}

Interior, main hall of das Kinderkrankenhaus.

Grey. The hospital is grey. Full of grey beds and grey floors and grey walls. Grey doors with silver handles that glint like a distant freedom. It has grey wiring that cuts a pattern of diamonds in its few windows. Grey: cups, pills, and the paddles of horse-hair brushes. Only grey water runs from its oxidized faucets. The people inside too. Grey.

The wall opposite the audience is lined with bunk beds. In the exact center of the grey stone wall, there is a small place where the stones have fallen, creating a small cavern. Above the entry a $\sum$ has been carved.

All children inside wear a grey tunic that is sealed in the back with a series of ties. Depending on how old the patient is, it falls anywhere between mid-calf all the way down to the ankle. On a few, it skims the floor. Their hair is cut identically as well, in a bob no longer than the bottom of their earlobes. At the midpoint of their skull, the hair is parted and fringe is cut in the front so that it falls right above the eyebrows. Unless the patient has coarse hair. In that case, the nurses shave the whole head clean. Even the eyebrows. Not the only extra abuse patients see for standing out, intentionally or not.

The children are playing. Or doing whatever activities we call play, no matter how silly or serious they may be. The children are.

Gnome enters, led by Dr. Schmetterling (the Doctor's hand on Gnome's shoulder). Stabat Mater.

After a pause to look around, Dr. Schmetterling: "Well, what do you think of your new home?"

Gnome: "It looks like the inside of a rock."

Dr. Schmetterling: "Well . . . that's where you can find a diamond, isn't it?"

the Shadow, rocking in place: "Die man, die man, die man, die man, die man, die man, die man, die man, die man, die man, die man, die man, die man, die man, die—"   Nix: "And fossils, and oil, and minerals, and geodes, and endoliths—"

Dr. Schmetterling: "Yes, children, yes. Enough. Peace please. Come now, quietly, and gather around. Meet our new friend."

Most of the children gather in a circle around Gnome with Doctor Schmetterling at the apex. A few children remain standing where they were before, though some of them are less engaged with their activity.

Dr. Schmetterling: "Well, what should we call this one, Eros?"

Eros, patting Gnome on the head three times: "Gnome. I think. Funny red. Clever red. I think."

Dr. Schmetterling: "Yes, I agree. Gnome. Another little gnome living inside this rock. [leaning down over Gnome] You will be called Gnome from now on."

Gnome: " 'Til when?"

Dr. Schmetterling, starting to move down the row of beds: "As long as you're here, [tapping a bunk] this is your place. Right here."

Gnome: "Where? Where?"

Dr. Schmetterling exits without looking back. The children disperse back to their activities, except for Cinders. Periodically, a child lets out a momentary shriek or extended single-note hum.

Cinders: "Das Kinderkrankenhaus."

Word appears [KINDERKRANKENHAUS].

Gnome: "What?"

Cinders: "That's here. Kin-der-kran-ken-haus. It's German."

Gnome, puzzled: "German?"

Cinders: "The name is German. The Germans love compound words."

Gnome: "What is that?"

Cinders: "Words made of more words. Words made of more than just one word."

Gnome: "Like a sentence?"

Cinders: "No."

Gnome: "So, words with more than one meaning?"

Cinders: "No—I mean, like butterfly is made of the word butter and the word fly. Kinderkrankenhaus is three words. [pointing to each part] Kinder meaning children, kranken meaning suffering, and haus meaning . . . house."

Gnome: "Childrensufferinghouse."

Cinders: "Yes, a hospital—for sick kids."

Gnome: "Why are we in a hospital?"

Cinders: "Because we're sick, of course. Terribly, terribly sick."

Gnome: "What's wrong with us?"

Cinders: "All sorts of things. Bright, gleaming things."

Gnome, reading: "Kinder crank in hows."

Cinders: "No, *kinder*. Kin. Derrr."

Gnome, sitting on the bunk: "Okay."

Cinders, coming closer: "Don't worry, Gnome. There's always a cure. You just have to want to find it."

Gnome, rolling on their side: "I'm not Gnome."

Cinders, laughs: "You are now. The doctor says so."

Cinders wanders away.

Gnome tosses and turns in the bunk, increasingly agitated. Finally, Gnome stands and says: "How can you cure something you cannot see? Isn't everything made visible through me?"

No one answers. Gnome approaches the Shadow, who is flapping their hands sporadically in front of their body.

Gnome: "What are you doing? Fighting invisible insides?"

Eros: "the Shadow. Don't talk much. No. Mmm."

Gnome: "No one can give me any answers around here."

Eros: "No, don't you know. Know-mmm?"

Gnome: "What makes you think I know anything?"

Eros: "What makes you think? I do."

Gnome, turning to other children: "Do you? Do any of you?"

Nix: "I do. I know any thing. It comes from chaos. Ex nihilo. Genesis. Creation. Procreation. Created from nothing . . ."

Gnome: "How can you make something from nothing?"

Cinders: "You take it in your hands. And you give it a name."

Gnome sits on the ground, starts to cry.

Eros: "Gnome, no. Know no mmm."

Cinders: "Why are you crying?"

Gnome: "I don't like it here."

Eros: "No. One does."

Gnome: "I want to go home."

Nix: "Home is where the heart is."

Gnome: "Where are my parents? Where are all the adults? I don't even know why I'm here. No one told me nothing."

Nix: "Oh, to be here, you must be really ill. Infirm. An epidemic nowadays. Sick, sick children."

Gnome: "How do you know?"

Nix: "That's what they [pointing to the only door] say. The doctors and soldiers and teachers and parents and people with official letters that give us our official names."

Gnome: "What are your official names?"

Nix: "Oh, in here, we are given many names. I am Nix, that is the Shadow, and Cinders. And that is Eros."

Gnome: "Are you saying errors?"

Cinders: "Eros. Air-*Rohs*."

Gnome, pointing to the door: "And they gave you those names?"

Nix: "Oh, no, there is a funny story behind each appellation. Nicknames. Or sobriquets. Or cognomen. Cog-no-men. Cog-gnome-n.

Word appears {COGNOMEN (together-name)}

"A name is how we gnomen, know men."

Cinders, interrupting: "You will have to figure it out or else you'll end up in the Loch."

Gnome: "What?"

Cinders: "Figure out why you're here."

Gnome: "No, what's the Lock?"

Eros: "Oh no, it is a place outside some. Where we don't know, Gnome. Mmm—no know mmm—maybe. Or . . ."

Nix: "We don't know what it means when the Doctor says it's where the disease ceases to be."

Gnome: "So you don't know. But you're still afraid of it."

Cinders: "They're afraid *because* they don't know."

Eros: "You are. Too!"

Cinders: "No, I'm not!"

Nix, quietly: "The children that go there never come back."

Gnome: "Sounds like the kids who don't have to come here. Kids that live without an official name. It sounds like that's where we want to be."

The other children are silent.

Gnome: "If you don't know something's wrong, then couldn't it be alright?"

The Shadow: "All right, all right, all right, all right, all right, ⫞ ."

Cinders: "Are you talking about yourself or the Loch?"

Gnome: "How can I ask about something I didn't know existed?"

Cinders: "Well, you do now."

Gnome: "You guys should give up on these goofy names. They're ridiculous. What are your real names?"

Eros: "Oh, Gnome, these. Names have real meaning."

Gnome: "You can't become whatever someone labels you. That name is not a part of you, like your nose."

Nix, slightly desperate: "Oh, no, yes, they are. Eros is right. The name becomes you. No misnomer. No mis-no-more. Miss-gnome-her."

Cinders: "Gnome, don't confuse Nix. We live within a narrow language. Names are everywhere but meaning is mall-able."

Nix: "Malleable! You mean malleable."

Cinders: "Malleable."

Nix, wandering away: "Malleable. Male-he-able. Mmm-ale-e-al. Mallet. Malicious . . ."

Gnome: "No, don't go Nix. [Nix continues off stage] I wanted to ask about the stories behind your names. Are they really funny?"

Cinders: "Depends on what you think is funny."

They stand in silence for a moment, not knowing what to say.

Gnome: "I'm sorry."

Cinders, shrugging: "You don't have to be sorry with me."

Gnome: "No, I just meant in general."

Cinders shrugs again.

Gnome: "Just trying to understand what's going on."

Cinders: "You will have to meet with Doctor Schmetterling soon. There is a personal session for each patient on their second day here. Maybe you'll listen when the Doctor gives you an answer."

Cinders walks away.

Gnome walks to a bed and lays down.

{curtain falls}

ACT I · scene 3

{curtain and lights rise}

Dr. Schmetterling and Gnome sit across from each other on grey steel chairs. The rest of the set is empty. They look at each other for a moment quietly before dialogue starts.

Dr. Schmetterling: "Do you know that I have a prognosis for you Gnome?"

Gnome: "No."

Dr. Schmetterling: "Do you know what that means?"

Gnome: "No."

Dr. Schmetterling: "It means I have figured out what is wrong in you. Once we know what is wrong, we can try to fix it."

Gnome doesn't answer.

Dr. Schmetterling, continuing: "It's like a label for your illness. And how to possibly treat your illness. Wouldn't you like to be better?"

Gnome: "Okay."

Dr. Schmetterling: "Do you want to know what your label is?"

Gnome: "I don't know."

Dr. Schmetterling: "It's important to know what you are, Gnome."

Gnome: "I'm not Gnome."

Dr. Schmetterling: "And you need to know that if I say this then it is true."

Gnome: "This or it?"

Dr. Schmetterling: "What?"

Gnome: "You know if I say *this* then *it* is true. This or it—which is true?"

Dr. Schmetterling: "It's the same thing."

Gnome: "This or it—same like that?"

Dr. Schmetterling: "No, that is totally different. This here, that there."

Gnome: "Both it though."

Dr. Schmetterling: "Could be."

Gnome: "So then one it is right and the other it is wrong. If this and that are different."

Dr. Schmetterling: "I suppose, if you speak opaquely. But not necessarily. Gnome, I will give you a precise definition—we doctors call it a diagnosis—and that will be it. And they both will be this. And so you will be."

Dr. Schmetterling makes a few notes in the records before her. Gnome watches her.

Words appear {GNOSIS (knowledge)}

Nix wanders on stage below the words.

Nix: "Noses. No-sis. Know-sis. *Gno*sis. Know-m. Gnome."

Words appear {PROGNOSIS (before-knowledge)}

Nix: "Prognosis. Progress-is. Pro-gnosis. Proactive. Reactive. Creative. Pro-creative. Pro-, pro-fessional. Pros and cons. Confessional."

Words appear {DIAGNOSIS (apart-knowledge)}

Nix, wandering back offstage: "Di-ag-no-sis. Die-a-gnosis. Dia-critic. Dia-gram . . ."

Gnome, looking at Dr. Schmetterling's name tag: "Is that your name?"

Dr. Schmetterling, glancing down momentarily: "Yes."

Gnome: "Dew-roth-ee?"

Dr. Schmetterling: "It's Dorothy."

Gnome: "Doorthy?"

Dr. Schmetterling: "Yes. But you can call me Doctor Schmetterling."

Gnome: "Not Doorthy?"

Dr. Schmetterling: "No, that would be inappropriate. It would indicate to others that we have a relationship that we do not have."

Gnome: "By calling you your name?"

Dr. Schmetterling: "I would appreciate if you showed me the appropriate respect and called me Doctor."

Gnome: "Okay."

Dr. Schmetterling: "See, Gnome, this is an excellent example of why you are here. You seem to not be able to understand what is appropriate and what is not appropriate."

Gnome: "I don't?"

Dr. Schmetterling: "No, you don't. I would say that you exhibit what is called *deviant social behaviors* and an inability to relate to your peers. Do you understand?"

Gnome: "No."

Dr. Schmetterling: "What don't you understand?"

Gnome: "What is deviant?"

Dr. Schmetterling: "Anything that is not up to accepted standards."

Gnome: "How am I supposed to know what the standards are?"

Dr. Schmetterling: "Through interactions with other people."

Gnome: "Which I am unable to do with my peers?"

Dr. Schmetterling: "Yes."

Gnome: "Because of my deviant behaviors?"

Dr. Schmetterling: "Yes."

Gnome: "Is the cure just saying the right words set in the right order at the right time?"

Dr. Schmetterling: "Yes, it very well could be."

Gnome: "Okay. This, that, and it. I will try to keep them straight."

Dr. Schmetterling: "Trying's not good enough, Gnome. The truth is I'm not sure you have the mental capacity to make the right decisions. You see, people must be able to understand concrete facts, like these are chairs [reaching down to touch a chair leg]. They also have to understand the symbolic, like what love means, or justice."

Gnome: "What does it mean?"

Dr. Schmetterling: "What, symbolic?"

Gnome: "No, love. Justice."

Dr. Schmetterling, sighing, frustrated: "You don't know what it means to love someone?"

Gnome: "I think I do. But I can't be sure I'm right."

Dr. Schmetterling: "Well, I think people like you might not be able to understand all of the symbolic cues human interaction includes. So you might not understand it completely. It requires imagination and a departure from the literal. You see, you need to be able to see all the subtle cues a person carries in their face and be able to derive meaning from it."

Gnome, concerned, staring intently at Dr. Schmetterling's face: "I didn't know I wasn't reading faces the right way. I guess I didn't know I was supposed to."

Dr. Schmetterling: "Yes, well, you wouldn't, would you? People like you don't understand those things. You'll see children here like you, without autonomy over their own minds. Children that have a hard time expressing themselves. Some that don't talk at all. The whole reason people speak is to kindle recognition of meaning in another. There is a madness in silence. You see, we are social creatures. We need each other. Silence takes everyone else away. Those who cannot communicate cannot be thinking rationally or symbolically. They are just feeling, not thinking creatures."

Gnome: "How do you know?"

Dr. Schmetterling: "How do I know what?"

Gnome: "What is happening inside their mind? If there is a language in there or not? I think I think in language."

Dr. Schmetterling: "You may, Gnome. You may not. I cannot know for certain. But I can deduce that if you are behaving in antisocial ways that your brain isn't functioning correctly."

Gnome, increasingly anxious: "I'm sorry. I just don't understand why you think that about me. Did my parents tell you something?"

Dr. Schmetterling closes a notebook: "We are almost at time here. But I will leave you with these parting thoughts. Firstly, no one blames you for any deficit you may possess. Some people are simply this way, either through birth or through accident. While you're here, we will work towards increasing your capacity for symbolic understanding and imagination."

Gnome, interrupting: "How? How will you know how good my imagination is?"

Dr. Schmetterling: "There are standards that we go by. Marks you will need to hit."

Gnome: "Okay. I will work very hard for you. I promise. I want to get out of here."

Dr. Schmetterling: "Gnome, everyone gets out of here eventually. This is not a jail. It's a place for healing. It's up to the patient to leave here either better or the same. Those are the two paths out of here."

Gnome: "Okay. Okay."

Dr. Schmetterling: "To start with, it would be good for you to think about how you use your words and how you are choosing to behave. How we use our words is important. They can be something that binds us together, or they can be solvents that rend us apart. You have to use them carefully and correctly in order fit in."

Gnome: "I'm scared I'll do it wrong."

Dr. Schmetterling: "Gnome [stern, as a reprimand]. Just do your best. I will be here to help. And remember, it's not like a single word can swallow the whole entire world."

Gnome swallows hard.

{lights fall and curtain lands on the stage heavily as the fire intensifies}

ACT I · scene 4

{the fire burns, grows
curtains rise
dark set
a bell rings
lights rise}

Children in their dormitory get up, with Gnome the last to roll out of bed.

Approaching a group of children, Gnome: "I'm starving. I haven't had anything to eat in days. When are they going to feed us?"

Eros: "You will. Eat when they want . . . SOMETHING. Oh, no, mmm, it's part. Of healing. Trying to kill the germ. Inside us. You know, mmm—starve. A cold feed. A fever."

the Shadow: "Fever—fee-fur. Fur. Fever. Free-ver. Fur-eve-r." [wanders off mumbling]

Gnome: "I'm starving."

Most of the children disperse to various activities across the dormitory. Doctor Schmetterling enters and walks around, observing different children. She writes notes about the children and occasionally the audience hears her notes—
    "Disruptive."
    "Repetitive."
    "Where there is no language, behavior becomes nonhuman."

Meanwhile—

Cinders: "You're not going to get any frühstück here."

Word appears {Breakfast}

Gnome: "How do you know these words?"

Cinders, shrugs: "I don't know. I just hear them and then I know them. [pause] I can teach you the words I know if you want."

Gnome: "Okay."

Cinders: "That's German but I think French is prettier. I could teach you that too. REGARDEZ!"

Gnome: "Okay. Either. Both."

Cinders: "Can't be both either and both."

Gnome: "Why not?"

Cinders: "It will help you to look at the parts of the word in order to understand the meaning. Like regardez—it is like any word that starts with re . . .

Prefix appears {RE- (go back)}

"as in to re-do something. And gardez is the same as our word guard.

Words appear {GUARD (watch over to protect or control)}

"So basically—it means look. REGARDEZ!"

Gnome: "Ra-gar-day."

Cinders: "Pretty good. Now tell me what sounds prettier—ich liebe dich or j'taime."

Words appear {ICH LIEBE DICH}

Words appear {J'TAIME}

Gnome: "I don't know."

Cinders: "Which one?"

Gnome: "Pretty?"

Cinders: "You have to choose!"

Gnome: "Okay, okay. The last one, I guess."

Cinders: "Yup, French. Told you. They both mean love. Liebe in German and aime in French."

Gnome: "Lie-be and mmm."

Cinders: "Liebe."

Gnome: "Lee-bah."

Cinders; "Pretty good. This could be fun. We could speak to each other in languages no one else knows. A whole bunch of languages at once."

Gnome: "Like our own secret code."

Cinders: "Yeah, but it might take a while. Besides pronunciation, there's all the weird sentence structures and things."

Gnome: "Why weird?"

Cinders: "Well, normally . . . Subject verbs something."

Gnome: "Subject verbs something?"

Cinders: "Yes, but en Deutsche, etwas verbietet das Thema. And en Francais, sometimes le sujet quelque chose verbes. With apostrophes."

the Shadow: "Apostrophe! ' Apostrophe! ' Apostrophe! '
[ad infinitum]"

Nix, across the room: "A one-way fire. Apostrophe. Alliteration.
EllipsissSibilance. Synecdoche. Schenectady."

Gnome remains silent.

Cinders: "Maybe it's better to focus on words instead of grammar. We can forget grammar."

Gnome: "What is that?"

Cinders: "What?"

Gnome: "Grammar."

Cinders: "It's just rules about how you use words."

Gnome: "I don't need that before I learn the words?"

Cinders: "No. We'll keep it simple—you'll learn how to name things before you'll learn how to use them."

Gnome: "But that's the problem Doctor Schmetterling thinks I have—using words before understanding the rules about how to use them."

Cinders: "That's what she told you yesterday?"

Gnome: "That I don't understand the rules—yes. I'm *deviant*."

Cinders, short laugh: "Yeah, I don't think anyone does. [looks at Gnome, and becomes more serious] I wouldn't worry about that. It's easy to learn rules, and if not, just to stay quiet. Other people here have it worse."

Gnome, looking at the Shadow shouting about apostrophes: "Like the Shadow?"

Cinders, turning towards the Shadow: "No, the Shadow's fine—always there for you. I'm talking about Python."

Gnome: "Which one is that?"

Cinders: "The smallest one—the one with the white hair."

Gnome: "Oh. What's wrong with Python?"

Cinders: "Knows too much. [smiles] Python is very quiet, always watching, but when Python talks—it's in a way that Doctor Schmetterling can't understand."

Gnome: "Like another language."

Cinders: "Yes. Exactly."

Gnome: "And that's a bad thing? To be quiet?"

Cinders: "It's bad to not have the Doctor understand you."

Gnome, after a pause: "What makes you think Python's smart? Maybe the language is just make-believe."

Cinders: "You'll see. Everything is a code. Python knows more than you do. Or me. Anyone here. I've seen Python read the future we carry in our skin. Read invisible things. Like time. Come on, I'll show you. Maybe Python can tell you how to get out of here."

Cinders takes Gnome by the hand and they head to the small cave situated in the middle of the dormitory's wall. Getting down on their knees, they crawl and disappear into the cave, below a solitary Σ carved at the pinnacle of its entrance.

{all stage lights die. The fire that rims the stage even dies once inside Python's cave, though its heat is still felt like a quickening.}

{lights rise.}

The stage is a single, windowless cave. Besides Python, the only thing inside the cave is a bowl set up on a tripod. Inside are different treasures: a frog, a dead mouse, the shed skins of different snakes, and the jeweled backs of beetle shells like diadems. Below the bowl of treasures, in the center of the tripod's legs is a stone. It exists in the exact center—of the tripod, of the cave, of KINDERKRANKENHAUS. Gnome and Cinders enter, the same characters but portrayed by adults. Their larger bodies occupy the small space awkwardly, they bend and stoop, above Python and the shrine. Python is small, tight-lipped, with white-blonde hair and the pallor of a corpse.

Python breathes steadily, audibly, with hands held ceremoniously above the bowl and does not seem to notice Cinders or Gnome have entered the cave. Python does not make eye contact.

Finally—

Gnome, holding hand across face: "Why does it smell so bad over here?"

Cinders: "Snakes. [points to pile] Python kills the ones that crawl in from the stone wall. They're attracted to the cool. Python hits them in the head with that rock. [points to the rock] I think it's got an almost sweet smell."

Gnome: "It's meat rotting."

Cinders: "Yes." [turns to Python] "Python, this is Gnome."

Python does not respond, does not move.

Cinders: "Gnome like an elf."

The cave begins to fill with smoke from the quieted stage. Cinders and Gnome cough, but Python inhales deeply. Vapors. A distant beat begins. Python begins mumbling numbers and letters of the alphabet slowly, enunciating like a child new to language.

Between the numbers, Cinders says—

> "Speak in poetry!"
> "god is a Number!"
> "Sleep in a special place and it will reveal special dreams."

Through the growing smoke, Python's growing numbers, and Cinders interjections, Gnome shouts—

"What's happening?"

Finally, Python, loudly: "Five, four, be, two, one, zarrow."

Gnome: "What?"

Python, eyes shut, shouting: "ZARROW! ZARROW!"

Outside the cave, Dr. Schmetterling: "Hello! What's going on in there?"

Python, opening eyes, looking towards the entrance: "No, O, no, 0!"

Cinders: "Oh no!"

A hand, the size of a German shepherd, enters the cave, feeling around.

Dr. Schmetterling, from outside: "Hello! Who's in there?"

Cinders: "Kinder."

Gnome, pressed against the wall of the cave: "Do you think the Doctor's mad?"

Cinders: "They hate nothing more than when we don't need them. They hate not being allowed in. Your mouth is a door, Gnome. Your tongue is the key."

Python: "Tung, tung. Zarrow!"

The hand grabs Gnome by the ankle and begins pulling towards the entrance, now an exit. Python looks at Gnome for the first time and says, just as Gnome is pulled into the outside,—

"No U Elf."

{lights die. Curtains fall.}

fire begins anew, with increased strength.

{curtains rise. Lights rise.}

Inside the dormitory, Dr. Schmetterling drags Cinders (now again child patient) and Gnome (again child patient) out of the cave by their ankles. They stand on either side of the $\sum$ carved into the wall, smoke softly billowing out between them, now gray in the light.

Dr. Schmetterling: "What were you doing in there?"

Gnome, to Cinders: "What did Python say? 'Know' or 'no'?"

Dr. Schmetterling: "I'm speaking to you! What were you doing in there?"

Gnome and Cinders remain silent.

Dr. Schmetterling, exasperated: "Look at me! Use your words! I expect an answer!"

Gnome and Cinders remain silent. Doctor Schmetterling grabs them each by their ear and pulls them towards the only door.

Dr. Schmetterling: "We will get some answers out of you (two/too). Wait here and do *not* move."

Dr. Schmetterling exits.

Gnome and Cinders wait, standing by the door.

Eventually, quietly, Gnome: "I don't understand how you think Python is so free when we're all stuck together inside KINDER-KRANKENHAUS."

Cinders: "No, no. Python is free—inside a mind without end. Haven't you felt the limits of your own mind? Its walls? Python's mind is as open as the nighttime sky. A place so deep no shadow can be cast. It can read everything. Even what we can't see."

Gnome remains silent.

Cinders, continuing: "It takes a special heart to read a space between; only one that is broken—*free*—can recognize itself inside the gap . . . The chasm."

Gnome: "Kazz-m?"

Cinders: "Chasm, chasm—open, an open, opening. Open my chest. [a finger like a buzzsaw] Brrrr."

{pause.}

Gnome, bitterly: "Night is all shadow."

Cinders: "No, a shadow can't cast a shadow. Like a snake, it has no belly button. No center, no place it was attached to. Always there. Just out of reach."

{pause.}

Gnome: "I don't know what fortune Python said to me."

Cinders: "Put the puzzle together."

Gnome: "What do you mean? Python's not saying anything. Nothing is there. No or Know and You and Elf because Python thinks I'm a gnome. And a bunch of zeroes."

Cinders: "Creatio ex nihilo."

Gnome: "What?"

Cinders: "What Nix said, my friend. What are all of the things that could possibly mean?"

Gnome, angrily: "What? What do you mean? This makes no sense!"

Cinders: "Move beyond the actual words, Gnome." [pause.] "Possibility, Gnomon. Cast no shadow. Silence, all possibility!"

Doctor Schmetterling re-enters the dormitory with a nurse. The nurse takes Cinders by the arm and exits the room. Doctor Schmetterling leads Gnome to an empty corner of the room and kneels down to be face-to-face.

Dr. Schmetterling: "Gnome. Do you think that this has been a good transition to the KINDERKRANKENHAUS?"

Gnome: "Transition?"

Dr. Schmetterling: "You realize you are here to get better, no?"

Gnome: "No! Yes! I do."

Dr. Schmetterling: "You must try to get better. You realize that, no? If not, there will consequences."

Gnome: "Yes, yes!"

Dr. Schmetterling: "Do you know what consequences are?"

Gnome, after a moment: "Not getting better?"

Dr. Schmetterling: "To say the least. Not getting better means you become diagnosed as something far worse than what you are now. We call it Lebensunwertes leben."

Words appear {LEBENSUNWERTES LEBEN (. . .)}

Gnome: "Is that something about love something love?"

Dr. Schmetterling: "What?"

Gnome: "Love?"

Dr. Schmetterling: "No, you're confused."

Gnome: "So, if I don't get better, then I get worse?"

Dr. Schmetterling: "Staying exactly the same is worse than getting worse. Not trying to get better, to get along with me and the others, is when you get worse. And you will have work harder. We know because of who you are, you will lack empathy. You will have difficulty forming normal relationships. But you have to try."

Gnome: "Like friends? I am! Cinders and me are friends."

Dr. Schmetterling: "You shouldn't be worried about friends. You should be worried about yourself and getting better. Friends like Cinders will only get you in trouble. Cinders is our oldest patient. And you don't get old at the KINDERKRANKENHAUS."

Word flashes.

Gnome: "Why not?"

Dr. Schmetterling: "We can't keep patients here forever, if they're not going to try and get better."

Gnome: "Where do they go? If they're still sick?"

Dr. Schmetterling: "You can't go anywhere besides here to get better. This is your one shot, Gnome. One shot to get better, to become a functioning member of society. And if you can't, then we can't just release you, out into the world, society, if you are socially inadequate. That doesn't make sense, does it?

Gnome: "I don't know. I'm not sure where people go if they're sick besides the hospital."

Dr. Schmetterling: "Well, there is one other place. It is deep and it is dark and it is an absence forever. You don't want to go there. I don't want to send you there. But if you misbehave, if you don't *try* to get better, then I will have no choice."

Gnome remains silent. Doctor Schmetterling looks at them for a second.

Dr. Schmetterling: "Be good, Gnome. Because of the severity of your case, you don't have many more opportunities to show me some improvement."

Gnome, near tears: "I will. I will try. I just don't know how to . . ."

Dr. Schmetterling: "You need to *listen* to what is being told to you. Or you will be locked inside yourself forever."

Doctor Schmetterling exits. When she's gone, Gnome whispers, terrified—

"The Lock. It's real."

ACT I · Scene 5

A shower of numbers. Heavy beat from off-stage (steady in timbre and magnitude). Mahler's Kindertotenlieder no. 5 begins. The dark stage is broken by a single spotlight on Python outside her cave, the sigma symbol directly above Python's head.

Python, slowly, enunciating exaggeratedly; "One, two, be, fore, five, six, seven, eight, nine, ten, eleven, twelve, thirteen, fourteen, fifteen, sixteen, . . . [until] 100."

Spotlight grows until stage lights, showing Gnome pacing, alternatively agitated and entranced, and moving to different point of the stage. Gnome pauses at a different spot to observe another child engaged in one of the following activities:

- Lining up objects in a row from tallest to smallest
- Seated on the ground, rocking back and forth
- Looking straight ahead, as if lost in thought
- Crying/making guttural noises
- Jumping up and down, screeching
- Frowning, trying to move away from Gnome
- Using a rock to draw numbers and letters on the cement wall

Approaching Cinders, Gnome: "The doctor told me what was wrong with me."

Cinders: "Yeah?"

Gnome: "Yeah."

Cinders: "Yeah, I know."

Gnome: "I don't know how to get better. I'm sick but I didn't know. I . . ."

Cinders: "What don't you understand? It's not about you. It's all in how others read you. That's what makes you ill. [Cinders pauses but Gnome does not reply so Cinders continues.] You see, your body is the word and your actions are the grammar. Too bad that what you mean to say and what people understand are two different things."

Gnome: "Cinders, I got to get out of here. I'm afraid this place might swallow me whole."

Nix, across the room: "A single word can swallow the world."

Gnome: "We're in trouble, Cinders. The doctor . . . [whispering] told me that they'll study us for a while, to see if it is possible to cure us, but, if not, they will send us to the Lock. There really is a Lock. You all were right. And I don't want to find out what's there."

Cinders: "[laughs]"

Gnome: "No, you don't understand. Dr. Schmetterling said it was deep and it was dark and it was an absence forever."

Cinders, laughs, defiant: "Deep and dark? Sounds the night to me. Sounds like a chance to spread out in every direction, once you're free from the spotlight of the sun. I'm not afraid of her Loch."

Gnome, angrily: "Well, you should be. You might not know everything like you think you do. Dr. Schmetterling said it was the opposite of the world. I'm don't want to be outside the world any more. I want to be so far in it that I'm the core that burns inside."

Cinders: "Gno—"

Gnome, angry: "No! I'm not your friend. I'm serious. I don't want to fiddle with puzzles. I want to get out of here. I want to be better."

{fire grows, climbing the velvet curtains, reaching out towards the orchestra and stage boxes. Lights rise across the stage.}

Chorus, spread across the **KINDERKRANKENHAUS** interior, engaged in various activities:

"A word, unfit even to name the cinder in the place of the memory of something else, and no longer referring back to it, how can a word ever present itself? The word, like the cinder, similar to her, comparable to the point of hallucination. Cinder, the word, is never found here, but there."

A gentle bell sounds.

{The children climb into their beds. Python enters the cave. The music and beat fade. The lights go off.}

Stage is backlit.

The type of light you find at night. A blackness outside of complete/pitch. It shifts as you near it, close onto it. It moves to an unattainable periphery. It is always moving as if imagined. That light you find in darkness, that is what will guide you through this night. Unsteady and out of reach, but always near enough to expose the deeper shadows.

Nix: "At night, dark makes the world flat."

the room is dark. In one corner, a child cries softly.

Eros, whimpering: "Mommy. Mom. Mum. Mum . . ."

A pause. The only sound is fire crackling and soft tears from Eros.

Cinders, rolling over and leaning towards Gnome's bunk, whispering: "Gnome."

Gnome doesn't move.

Cinders, a little louder: "Gnome."

Gnome doesn't move.

Cinders, louder still: "Gnome!"

Gnome doesn't move.

Cinders: "I know you want answers. I think I know how to get you out of here."

A pause, then turning, Gnome: "How?"

intermission
{between   let go}

ACT II · scene 1

{the fire is now a raging conflagration framing center stage. Smoke gathers on the ceiling like an awful omen cloud.}

Chorus:

"How would the purest of the pure, the worst of the worst, the panicked blaze of the all-burning, put forth some monument, even were it a crematory? Some stable, geometric, solid form, for example, a pyramis that guards the trace of death?"

Nix: "Pyramis is a honey cake that helps you stay awake."

Chorus:

"If the all-burning destroys up to its letter and its body, how can it guard the trace of itself and
[half the children say "breach", half say "broach"]
breach/broach a history where it preserves itself in losing itself?"

A shower of numbers. Heavy beat from off-stage (steady in timbre and magnitude).

Dark stage, single spotlight on Python.

Python, slowly, enunciating exaggeratedly, drawing circles in the air with free hand: "be, 1, 4, 1, 5, 9, 2, 6, 5, be, 8, 9, 7, 9, be, 2, be, 8, 4, 6, 2, 6, 4, be, be, 8, be, 2, 7, 9, 5, 0, 2, 8, 8, 4, 1, 9, 7, 1, 6, 9,be, 9, 9, be,7 ,5 ,1, 0, 5, 8, 2, 0, 9, 7, 4, 9, 4, 4, 5, 9, 2, be, 0, 7, 8, 1, 6, 4, 0, 6, 2, 8, 6, 2, 0, 8, 9, 9, 8, 6, 2, 8, ,0 ,be 4, 8, 2, 5, be, 4, 2, 1, 1, 7, 0, 6, 7, 9, 8, 2, 1, 4, 8, 0, 8, 6, 5, 1, be, 2, 8, 2, be, 0, 6, 6, 4, 7, 0, 9, be, 8, 4, 4, 6, 0, 9, 5, 5, 0, 5, 8, 2, 2, be, 1, 7, 2, 5, be, 5, 9, 4, 0, 8, 1, 2, 8, 4, 8, 1, 1, 1, 7, 4, 5, 0, 2, 8, 4, 1, 0, 2, 7, 0, 1, 9, be, 8, 5, 2, 1, 1, 0, 5, 5, 5,

9, 6, 4, 4, 6, 2, 2, 9, 4, 8, 9, 5, 4, 9, be, 0, be, 8, 1, 9, 6, 4, 4, 2, 8, 8, 1,
0, 9, 7, 5, 6, 6, 5, 9, be, be, 4, 4, 6, 1, 2, 8, 4, 7, 5, 6, 4, 8, 2, be, be, 7,
8, 6, 7, 8, be, 1, 6, 5, 2, 7, 1, 2, 0, 1, 9, 0, 9, 1, 4, 5, 6, 4, 8, 5, 6, 6, 9,
2, be, 4, 6, 0, be, 4, 8, 6, 1, 0, 4, 5,
4, be, 2, 6, 6,4, 8, 2, 1, be, be, 9, be, Dr. Schmetterling, in soft light,
6, 0, 7, 2, 6, 0, 2, 4, 9, 1, 4, 1, 2, 7, enters the background, stage
be, 7, 2, 4, 5, 8, 7, 0, 0, 6, 6, 0, 6, left, observing Python with pen
be, 1, 5, 5, 8, 8, 1, 7, 4, 8, 8, 1, 5, 2, and notepad [overlapping dia-
0, 9, 2, 0, 9, 6, 2, 8, 2, 9, 2, 5, 4, 0, logue]: "Nonsense, utter non-
9, 1, 7, 1, 5, be, 6, 4, be, 6, 7, 8, 9, sense."
2, 5, 9, 0, be, 6, 0, 0, 1, 1, be, be, 0,
5, be, 0, 5 . . ."

Spotlight finds a group of children in far corner of stage, simultaneous
to Python's counting. Overlapping.

Cinders, to group: "Do you know what this symbol is?"

Nix: "Three!"

Eros: "Mmm, no, A-okay!"

Gnome, from outside the group, peevishly: "Asshole!"

Some members of the chorus giggle.

Nix: "Which one is right?"

Cinders: "Depends . . . three or it's okay you're an asshole."

Chorus giggles. Gnome, unimpressed, wanders away into the darkness.

Cinders, following, calling out: "Gnome! Gnome! [catches up to Gnome. Spotlight follows.] Do you want to still learn words with me today?"

Gnome: "I thought you were going to tell me how to get out of here. I've been waiting and I'm hungry and I'm tired."

Cinders: "I am, I am going to show you. I have to teach you how to do it though. It doesn't just happen. It takes time."

Gnome: "Time is moving. It is moving with us and it is moving away from us. I need to keep up."

Cinders doesn't respond.

Gnome: "I don't know why you think you're fit to be teacher here. You're in the same position as I am."

Cinders: "Well, I'm older."

Gnome: "So what?"

Cinders: "So, I've lived longer, learned more things."

Gnome: "I think you're full of yourself."

Cinders, hurt: "I am, I am just trying to help. I thought we were friends."

Gnome: "Why? Why would you think that?"

Cinders: "I don't know—"

Gnome, interrupting: "I just want to get better so I can get out of here. I don't want to be friends with people who just play games and get me in trouble."

Cinders: "You're not in trouble."

Gnome: "For someone who only cares about messages and reading situations, I don't think Doctor Schmetterling could make it more clear. We are all in trouble unless we get better. I told you! The Lock is real."

Cinders: "You can't even tell me what das Loch is."

Gnome: "That doesn't make it less real!"

Cinders doesn't respond.

Gnome: "I don't have time to waste. I need to move. Time is measured in movement. How far we move. Each second forward towards the cure moves me further away from nothing."

Cinders: "A cure? It isn't what you think, Gnome. It's not a magic potion. I'm trying to show you—"

Gnome: "No! Unless you're going to tell me how to get out of here, keep your mysteries to yourself! I'm done playing."

Gnome exits.

{lights die}

{curtain falls}

ACT II · Scene 2

{curtains, lights rise}

{fire burns}

The children form a line in front of a table, behind which stands Doctor Schmetterling and the nurse. They are handing out chunks of grey bread on a grey platter. The entire KINDERKRANKENHAUS waits restlessly in line, pushing, animated. Ravenous. Ravage, us!

Dr. Schmetterling: "Patience, Kinder, patience! One at a time, one at a time."

the Shadow: "Patients, patients, patients. Patients. Patients."

Gnome, to Nix, waiting in line: "The way the Doctor talks, doesn't it sound like a song? Or maybe something much more important. Maybe more like a hymn."

the Shadow: "Him? Hmm? Him? Him? Hmm?"

Nix shrugs.

After receiving their bread, most of the children sit at another table that has been set up near their bunks and they eat esuriently with their hands. Cinders and Gnome sit separated from each other. Python returns to the cave. Some of the chorus make guttural noises or flap their hands. Some are assisted by the nurse. Doctor Schmetterling stands at the head of the table, observing the children, taking notes.

Gnome finishes the bread and then gets up, approaching Doctor Schmetterling.

Gnome: "Doctor Schmetterling, I was wondering, do you know how we learn to remember? Is it a skill we acquire as babies, like eating or talking? Or do our memories not form before we have the words to describe them?"

Dr. Schmetterling: "I'm not sure, Gnome. You need to return to your seat."

Gnome: "I was wondering 'cause I'm trying to figure out if I think in language or not. And I know I can't remember being a baby, before I spoke."

Dr. Schmetterling: "We can't communicate with babies, Gnome. So we don't know. Now return to your seat. Don't make me ask again."

Gnome returns to the table.

After the children finish, Doctor Schmetterling dismisses them from the table and they spread across the KINDERKRANKENHAUS into various activities, play, as the Doctor and nurse fold up and re-move the tables from the room. When they return, Doctor Schmetter-ling moves around the room, taking notes. After a few moments, Gnome approaches her.

Gnome: "Why is Python allowed in the cave?"

Dr. Schmetterling, looking up from her pad: "That little hole? Well . . . Python's not bothering anyone there."

Gnome: "It can't be good to be apart from everyone else. If we're here to learn how to be better socially."

Dr. Schmetterling: "Gnome, some people are beyond saving. They will never get better. So we let them bide their time."

Gnome: "So you're okay with Python sitting in there alone? Just think-ing all day."

Dr. Schmetterling: "Python's not thinking."

Gnome: "What do you mean?"

Dr. Schmetterling: "Just sitting. Not thinking."

Gnome: "You can't not think."

Dr. Schmetterling: "You don't think so?"

Gnome: "No. People are always thinking, even if it's about nothing important."

Dr. Schmetterling: "Well, that's not true for some people. There's no thought."

Gnome: "Like being asleep?"

Dr. Schmetterling: "I guess."

Gnome: "How do you know?

Dr. Schmetterling: "Look. [points to the cave] There is nothing there. No expression of thought. Just silence."

Gnome: "Python knows numbers, some alphabet. That pointy E."

Dr. Schmetterling: "Mmm? Letters and numbers, only in random order. It becomes nonsense. An echo is not evidence of knowledge. It's hollow. Like a cave. Right words in the right order at the right time, right, Gnome?"

Gnome: "Right."

Doctor Schmetterling moves, and resumes her notes. Gnome follows her.

After a moment, Gnome: "But what if Python is trying to tell us something? Would you know what was being said?"

Dr. Schmetterling: "What?"

Gnome: "Do you feel like numbers and letters, the way you move even, could be a message too? Outside of language?"

Dr. Schmetterling: "What are you talking about?"

Gnome: "Python told me something and I'm trying to figure out what it means."

Dr. Schmetterling: "If it came from Python, it means nothing because Python does not understand how to communicate with us."

Gnome: "With us."

Dr. Schmetterling: "Gnome, shouldn't you be playing with your friends?"

Gnome: "Is that what you would like me to do?"

Dr. Schmetterling: "Leave Python alone and go play with your friends."

Gnome: "I don't have any friends."

Dr. Schmetterling, turning to look at Gnome: "You're not friends with Cinders anymore?"

Gnome: "I was never friends with Cinders, Doctor Schmetterling."

Dr. Schmetterling: "Oh really? Hmm. Okay. Well, that's good. Now you can focus on making friends who will be good influences."

Gnome: "Who do you want me to be friends with?"

Dr. Schmetterling: "Gnome, I can't choose your friends. Go and try to play with friends your age."

Gnome: "Is being the same age important?"

Dr. Schmetterling: "It's what people normally do."

Gnome: "Okay, I will go make friends, Doctor Schmetterling."

Gnome leaves Doctor Schmetterling and approaches Eros. Without looking directly at Eros, Gnome asks: "Eros, will you be my friend?"

Eros: "Oh, Gnome."

Gnome: "Okay?"

Eros: "Oh. Mmm, Gnome. Okay, mmm. Aren't we? Already?"

the Shadow: "All ready? All ready? All ready? All ready?"

Gnome: "I don't know."

Eros: "Oh, mmm. I-mmm. Thought, so?"

Gnome: "Well, if you think so, then so it must be."

Nix: "I think therefore I am. Cogito, ergo sum."

> Words appear [COGITO ERGO SUM]
>
> Words appear [I think | therefore | I am]
>
> Word appears [sum]

Eros: "Oh, mmm. Okay."

Gnome: "Okay."

Eros: "Mmm. Gnome as a friend you know. You can not be. Friends with Schmet? Terling—Oh."

Gnome: "Hmmm?"

Nix: "Do you want to hear how we got our names?"

Gnome, turning back and forth between Nix and Eros: "What? I mean yes, I do, but what did Eros say?"

Nix: "There's funny stories behind all our names. the Shadow, mine, Cinders, Python. Sweet, hesitant Eros. With the speech impediment sounds like Errors. But no, it's because Eros found a letter one day. It was on the floor, like an accident, occident, oracle. Picked it up and opened it. Pulled out words like Kinder, Toten, Lebens, Unwertes.

Words appear [KINDER

TOTEN

LEBENS

UNWERTES]

And on the cover, a big red stamp that read ERO. Beneath it said Eugenics Record Office. When Doctor Schmetterling found out, she demanded that we give her ERO's back. E-R-O's. Eros. Air-rose."

Gnome: "What do you think that means?"

Nix: "What?"

Gnome: "That word?"

Nix: "What?"

Gnome: "Eugenics."

Word appears [EUGENICS]

Nix: "Eugenics. You-genetic. You frenetic. Eu-phemism. You phonet-ics."

Cinders, approaching: "It means the good birth."

Words appear [EUGENICS (good-genes)]

Gnome: "Go away Cinders. No one wants you here."

Cinders: "I'm just trying to help. Okay?"

Gnome: "No, I have no idea what that means."

Cinders: "Helfen, aider."

Gnome: "No, what the good birth records office means? They keep track of births?"

Cinders: "Right, keeping track of people who were born with good genes. And who weren't."

Nix: "Disease. Dis-eased. Disability. Dis-able."

Gnome: "Okay, so? We know we're sick."

Cinders: "Do you know what those others words mean?"

Gnome: "Children, life, something."

Cinders: "Yes, unwertes. Wertes means worthy. So, unwertes, in-digne."

Word appears [UNWERTES (not-worthy)]

Gnome: "Children with unworthy lives."

No one answers.

Gnome: "But the Doctor is going to make us better! We just have to—"

Eros: "Oh, no. Mmm. See? Doctors gave us this. Names. Mmm. Er-rors."

Gnome is silent for a moment.

Gnome: "I don't know what to believe."

Cinders: "You know you don't have to take their name. You only take it if you really own it."

Gnome: "How can we own it when words get lost in the air?"

Cinders, strongly: "When the proper word does not exist, when it gets lost or hidden, you make a new one. You take it in your hands and you give it a name. And then you add it to all possibilities of understanding."

Gnome, quietly: "Something new."

{curtain falls}

ACT II · scene 3

{lights rise}

{the fire yawns in great terrible breathes}

A bell chimes and the children rise from their bunks. Doctor Schmetterling enters from the only door (entrance/exit). Gnome approaches the Doctor.

Dr. Schmetterling: "Good morning, Gnome."

Gnome: "Good morning, Doctor Schmetterling."

Dr. Schmetterling: "How are you feeling this morning?"

Gnome: "I don't feel great."

Dr. Schmetterling: "Why is that?"

Gnome: "I didn't sleep well last night. I kept having bad dreams."

Gnome had dreamt of a black, gaping hole, full of wet, foul-smelling crags along it's walls. Of fire. Of a horrible hole like a mouth that chewed forever, its tongue like a fork.

Dr. Schmetterling: "Well, I'm sorry about that. [pause] You know it would be appropriate to ask me how I was feeling this morning, right?"

Gnome: "Oh, I'm sorry. How are you feeling this morning, Doctor Schmetterling?"

Dr. Schmetterling: "Very well. Thank you."

Gnome: "Thank you."

Dr. Schmetterling: "You don't need to say thank you when I thank you."

Gnome: "Yes, okay. I'm sorry."

Dr. Schmetterling: "No need to be sorry—just be better. Now go ahead, Gnome. I don't want to have to continually remind you to play with other people your own age. Remember what we said about age?"

Nix: "What traps us within our body. Age, age, sage, page, suff-rage, suffer-rage, suffer-age . . ."

Gnome: "I was hoping I could ask you a question."

Dr. Schmetterling: "Then ask it, Gnome."

Gnome: "I don't know how to word it."

Dr. Schmetterling: "Gnome, I don't have time for these games. What does it have to do with?"

Gnome: "The hospital. The **KINDERKRANKENHAUS**."

> Word appears.

Dr. Schmetterling: "What about it?"

Gnome: "Well, I . . . um . . ."

Dr. Schmetterling: "Well, go ahead!"

Gnome, looking into the Doctor's eyes: "What do they do at the ERO?"

Dr. Schmetterling: "What?"

Gnome: "The Eugenics Records Office."

Dr. Schmetterling: "Where did you hear about this?"

Gnome: "I don't know."

Dr. Schmetterling, after a pause: "The ERO is my boss. I answer to them."

Gnome: "But what do they do?"

Dr. Schmetterling: "They help keep us free from social ills. They help take care of people who cannot help themselves. Who do not contribute."

Gnome: "Who is us?"

Dr. Schmetterling: "Gnome. Sometimes a woman will have a baby, a baby that is not normal. Either through their bodies or through their minds. You need someone to help that woman help her child. Or else that child becomes a burden to society. So the ERO sends them to KINDERKRANKENHAUS to see if we can teach them to keep their hands from waving, to stop up the jumble of vowels that fall from their mouths, inarticulate. And we either help them or have to figure out how to keep them from burdening others. You have to learn how to get along with everyone. Even if you don't want to. Because if you can't . . . I will have to send you away. [pause] Do you understand Gnome? Do you see? We are very similar in some ways. Because I, too, have no empathy. I will do what I have to for what's best."

Gnome: "I have empathy, Doctor Schmetterling."

Dr. Schmetterling: "Not that I've seen."

Gnome: "Just because you haven't see it, doesn't make it not real."

Dr. Schmetterling: "Gnome, you are sick whether you believe it or not."

Gnome: "That's not my name!"

Dr. Schmetterling, sighing: "I'm tiring of this conversation. The ERO helps people, hopefully while they're still children, because they don't know they're sick."

Gnome: "I don't know if I am sick."

Dr. Schmetterling: "Well, you do now."

Gnome: "It's just—it seems like hubris to try and predict the potential of any person."

Word appears [HUBRIS]

Dr. Schmetterling: "How do you know what that word means?"

Gnome: "Which?"

Dr. Schmetterling, pointing: "Hubris."

Gnome: "I don't know. I heard it once and then I knew it."

Dr. Schmetterling: "So, do you think your life is a Greek tragedy? Hmmm? Are you feeling bad for yourself, Gnome?"

Gnome: "No. No, it is not a tragedy."

Dr. Schmetterling: "No, it isn't. Everyone has problems. But you just need to listen to me. What am I always telling you?"

Gnome: "To make friends. And I have."

Dr. Schmetterling: "Yes. But what else? What is the most important part to healing you?"

Gnome is silent.

Dr. Schmetterling: "The important part about finding friends, about forming normal relationships, is that you are communicating properly. You are providing proof that you are able to function in a society, in a shared reality, and that is contingent on how well you use your words. How unfathomable would the mute mind be that thinks without language!"

Gnome: "I don't think the mind can ever be mute."

Dr. Schmetterling: "Look around, Gnome. This room is full of mute minds."

Gnome: "No! No. No, those are timid tongues. Broken tongues. Twisted tongues and confusion. I'm still not sure how anyone communicates at all—when people say things they don't mean, they state opinions like facts, they say things they think mean one thing but are really its opposite. Like when people talk about space, I realize they don't really mean space—vastness, infiniteness, nothingness. They don't mean black or lack of color or light. They mostly mean a container we're in, imaginary, between a Heaven and a Hell—the things inside it, not the space, the places between us. And then there are words that have multiple meanings, opposite meanings. Like cleave. Or funny. And then the words that are shaped differently depending on where they are supposed to live in a sentence, as either a verb or a noun. It drives me crazy. No. Speech . . . words are the last things that should show you what is inside a mind."

Dr. Schmetterling: "Well, what then?"

Gnome, surprised: "What then what?"

Dr. Schmetterling: "What would separate us from the animals—what chasm? What puddle? What would you have us use to prove our intelligence?"

Gnome: "Why would you have to prove intelligence?"

Dr. Schmetterling: "Because, Gnome! Because we need something to gauge how effective a person will operate in society. Words are the only tool we have. Communication. You cannot exist just for yourself. People want your words. And they want them in a specific order. I'm telling you, Gnome, look at me, I am telling you that you need to make me, and only me, feel like I can understand what is happening inside your mind. I need proof. More importantly, you need proof. Or else the ERO will send you someplace else. And it isn't home. It's a nowhere broken people go."

Gnome, starting to cry: "It doesn't make sense. It doesn't seem fair."

Dr. Schmetterling: "Who do you think deserves that justice? You?"

The Shadow: "Just us, just us, just us, just us, just us . . ."

Dr. Schmetterling: "Nothing is given to you in this life. Sometimes, for no reason, you will have to prove yourself. In the end, you will leave but where you go is your choice. But everyone goes somewhere. Just ask your friend Cinders."

Gnome: "Cinders?"

Dr. Schmetterling: "Yes, haven't you been told yet? Cinders will be leaving us tomorrow. Moving on. Onward and upward."

Dr. Schmetterling turns and walks towards other children, taking out the clipboard.

Gnome looks around, lost, as the curtain falls.

{fire screams. The ceiling starts to fall. The orchestra pit blazes like a sacred pyre.}

ACT II · scene 4

{curtains rise}

Gnome rushes to Cinders. The other children border the stage in the background, just outside the light. Outside the stage, the fire has taken over the entire theater. It shines like the inside of the sun. Or the World. Against the flames, everything grey now looks white.

Gnome: "Cinders!"

Cinders, turning towards Gnome: "What?"

Gnome, breathless: "Are you really leaving soon?"

Cinders: "Yes, Doctor Schmetterling says I outgrew this place. I'm getting too old for KINDERKRANKENHAUS."

Word appears.

Gnome: "Outgrew? You outgrew?"

Cinders: "If you believe in the word disability. The word only exists with your faith."

Gnome: "Where are you going? Are you cured? Or . . ."

Cinders: "You always make me repeat myself. This means nothing. No thing. A doctor, carrying a clipboard, making notes, behind these walls, inside this rock, king of the hill, calls this, all this, some thing and suddenly it's something. That name . . . the word draws a line like a blade. The chasm, remember, brrrr cutting open my chest? We're on the wrong side. But, really, in reality, we're still the same. We are the same. No thing. Nothing. The difference is a tongue licking the air."

Gnome starts crying.

54

Cinders: "What? Why are you sad?"

Gnome: "I'm not sad. I'm angry with you."

Cinders: "What do you mean? I didn't think you would care. I thought you hated me."

Gnome: "I don't want you to go away. I'm scared."

Cinders: "Don't be scared. I'm not scared. There is no better option. Besides, you were right, I shouldn't be a teacher. I'm not smart. I'm normal but not normal enough. They will let me go soon only because I know what they know—how to pretend to understand the nonsense, how to make other people feel comfortable and important. I know there are things I cannot say openly. I know that there are mysteries that I have not come close to understanding. I will miss being near them. I think some of the patients here understand more about those mysteries. They live closer to them—inside them maybe. I think they live beyond language."

Gnome: "So, for them, language went away like a tail we no longer need."

Cinders: "Yes, exactly—like a tale we no longer need."

Gnome: "You don't think we need it? Words?"

Cinders: "No, I think some people do. Most people. They want to feel like they can really understand something. But I don't think that you can ever really read a mind. I don't think you can fully know something with something as limiting as words. There are too many contradictions. Too many rules. They don't allow for the possibility of infinity."

Gnome: "But doesn't that make you sick?"

Cinders: "I'm told I do something, or maybe I do some things, wrong, in some sense. Some things other people would not do."

Gnome: "That doesn't make you sick. It doesn't make you sick to try and make something new."

Cinders, shrugging: "They say it does."

Gnome: "But are you? Really?"

Cinders: "I don't know, Gnome."

Gnome: "How do you know when something is wrong with you? When other people say so?"

Cinders: "What's real is real to you. You have to know yourself."

The sigma starts to burn in the background, in the center of a dark stage.

Gnome: "Zarrow!"

Cinders: "What?"

Gnome: "Zarrow, zero! I just had a thought—you know, a zero doesn't have to be a zero. A Nothing. It can be the circle you draw around yourself for protection. You can grow inside nothingness, within exception."

Cinders: "Buff out words. Labels."

Gnome: "Create a new language. Know yourself. Define yourself."

Cinders: "There it is."

Gnome: "What?"

Cinders: "The answer to all your questions. Il y a une réponse—es gibt eine Antwort—the answer! It there is! It gives!"

Gnome: "How should we do it?"

Cinders: "What?"

Gnome: "How can we destroy language? How do we do that?"

Cinders: "I suppose you take out the center."

Gnome: "How will we understand each other? Or understand our-selves?"

Cinders, shrugging: "Ask Python. I don't know. But do you really think we only know ourselves through language? Kill language. And we will have to know ourselves, not in terms of what we have been or might be, but through simply being. [grabs Gnome by the shoulders, points to Gnome's heart] Ici. Hier. The wrath of that awful metrognome. [laughs]"

Gnome: "How do you think without words?"

Cinders: "Are we going to do this?"

Gnome: "Yes, let's destroy this haus and build our own. Wrap infinity inside."

Cinders smiles.

Gnome: "So, how do we do it? How do we kill language?"

Cinders: "I think you take each word, each movement, each moment of time, and look at it from all sides. String them together or break them apart until you have created the meaning you want to see. What someone says to you, about you, is only as powerful as the meaning you give to it."

Gnome: "Okay. Okay. I will try. I want to. Let's burn this down."

Cinders: "Each new word a spark."

Gnome: "Each word a destruction!"

Cinders: "Each word something new!"

Gnome: "Try to think of something you couldn't describe."

[ABSTRACTIONS]

Gnome: "Do you see it?"

Cinders: "Nonsense?"

Nix: "Chaos, chaos, chasm . . ."

Cinders: "Look around! It already is! Are you still scared?"

Gnome, smiling, grabbing Cinders hand: "No!"

Nix: "I will cloak you (two/too). Like a coat, jacket, blanket . . . My Gnomon, even at night you cast a shadow."

Cinders: "Yes, come with us Nix. And Eros, and the Shadow. Someone get Python. Everyone, we're going to break free from all this."

The children rush around the stage, helping each other get in a group around Cinders and Gnome. The fire has almost eaten the whole building, save the very center of the stage, where the chorus flanks Cinders and Gnome like tableau of supplicants until Python joins them, held aloft, like the holy apex the whole mass aches toward. The intensity of the light has washed away almost all features besides the darkest outline. Black and mainly a piercing white.

Doctor Schmetterling flies in, frantic: "Oh, no! What is happening? Kinder! Kinder, what is going on? Gnome!"

Various members of the chorus:

- Cries and moans
- "Goodbye Doctor!"
- "Bye-bye!" or "The by-and-by!"
- "Nach oben!" or "Knock open!"
- "The Lock is here!" pressing their palms to their chests.

Over the roar of the flames, Gnome: "Come with us, Doorthy!"

Dr. Schmetterling: "Where are you going?"

Cinders: "Power is an illusion, Doctor!"

Dr. Schmetterling: "Child! Kind! Come here!"

Gnome: "Doctor is just a name! Come with us! Outside of language."

Dr. Schmetterling, the flames moving over her feet: "No! No! You need to come with me. Hurry!"

Cinders: "She will not join us, even if she is one of us. Kinder. Kinder."

Gnome: "Doorthy! Come with us! We can save you! There is nothing wrong with you!"

She does not move. The fire catches on her grey tunic, and then the bottom of her blunt bob feathers out in flame. As Doctor Schmetterling's prepubescent body is enveloped in flame, Cinders calls out: "Don't worry, Doctor. I have read many gods. I can speak for them all. There there is no pain."

Gnome: "Doorthy! She is still one of us!"

Cinders: "We can't save her, Gnome! We have to go now! Everyone, on the count of three, jump into the unknown."

Gnome turns panicked to watch what Doorthy will do. Before she completely disappears behind the wall of fire, Doctor Schmetterling reaches her arm up to what is left of the ceiling and forms a circle with her thumb and forefinger, leaving the other three pointed to the sky.

Python counts: "One, two . . . be!"

And they jump.

ACT II · scene GANZ ZULETZT

{the fire at the front of the stage has died. All is ash.}

outdoors, night sky. The other children are scattered among the stars by the wind.

Cinders and Gnome enter holding hands, under spotlight. There is the sound of waves crashing on a rough-edged shore.

Python, like Sirius, brightest star in the sky, serious, counts softly: "won, too, be, fore, I've, six . . ."

the Shadow, unseen against the sky: "Sicksicksicksicksicksicksicksicks . . ."

". . . 'ive, be, fore, won, too, 'ive, won, to, be, for, fore, I've, be, one, too, be, sic, $\{\{\infty, \pi\}\}$."

Gnome: "You know, I'm very lucky to have met you."

Cinders: "Luck? Do you think this is luck?"

Gnome: "I guess. In some form. In the same way all of this is real. In some form or another."

Cinders: "Well, in that case, I'm happy to know you too."

Gnome: "I wish we could have helped Doorthy."

Cinders, shrugging: "She wanted to stay. You can only help those who help themselves."

They move against the wind, further from KINDERKRANKEN-HAUS.

Cinders, pointing out along the edge of the stage: "Look—Il y a là cendra."

Words appear [there are the cinders there].

Words appear [LANGUAGE: the nothingness which presents itself materially].

Gnome: "Regardez—", pointing to Cinders heart, "there are Cinders here."

Cinders: "This is what I've been trying to say to you."

{a guttural grawlix punctures the air
then silence}

Das Ende

Jesi Bender is an artist from Upstate New York. She is the author of *The Book of the Last Word* from Whisk(e)y Tit, 2019. Her shorter work has been nominated for a Pushcart, Best of the Net, and Best Small Fictions, and can be seen in *The Rumpus*, *ellipsis*, and *Split Lip*, among other places. She also helms KERNPUNKT Press, a home for experimental writing.

BLANK PAGE BOOKS

are dedicated to the memory of Royce M. Becker,
who designed Sagging Meniscus books from 2015–2020.

They are:

IVÁN ARGÜELLES
THE BLANK PAGE

JESI BENDER
KINDERKRANKENHAUS

MARVIN COHEN
BOOBOO ROI
THE HARD LIFE OF A STONE, AND OTHER THOUGHTS

GRAHAM GUEST
HENRY'S CHAPEL

JOSHUA KORNREICH
CAVANAUGH
SHAKES BEAR IN THE DARK

STEPHEN MOLES
YOUR DARK MEANING, MOUSE

M.J. NICHOLLS
CONDEMNED TO CYMRU

PAOLO PERGOLA
RESET

BARDSLEY ROSENBRIDGE
SORRY, I BROKE YOUR PROMISE

CHRISTOPHER CARTER SANDERSON
THE SUPPORT VERSES

CPSIA information can be obtained
at www.ICGtesting.com
Printed in the USA
BVHW071529141221
624009BV00010B/1034